D0129082

# About this book

Almost everything that happens on earth involves motion. Worms burrow in the soil, and plants unfold their leaves and flowers. Air itself vibrates, and enables us to hear. Objects move in many different ways, with the help of springs, wheels, weights, magnets and electricity. You can find out how super these movements are by doing the experiments in this book. If you are not familiar with something you need for an experiment, look on p.6 for an explanation. Always read 'Laboratory procedure' on p.7 before you start an experiment.

# Contents

Cover illustration Tom Stimpson

Series editor Wendy Boase
Designer Alan Baron

Copyright © 1982 by Walker Books Ltd

First published in Great Britain in 1982 by Methuen Children's Books Ltd, in association with Walker Books.

All rights reserved. No part of this book may be reproduced or utilized in any form or by any means, electronic or mechanical, including photocopying, recording or by any information storage and retrieval system, without permission in writing from the Publisher. Inquiries should be addressed to Lothrop, Lee & Shepard Books, a division of William Morrow & Company, Inc., 105 Madison Avenue, New York, New York 10016.

Printed in Italy.
First U.S. Edition
1 2 3 4 5 6 7 8 9 10

Library of Congress Catalog Card Number 82-80990

ISBN 0-688-00976-X (pap.)
ISBN 0-688-00971-9 (lib. bdg.)

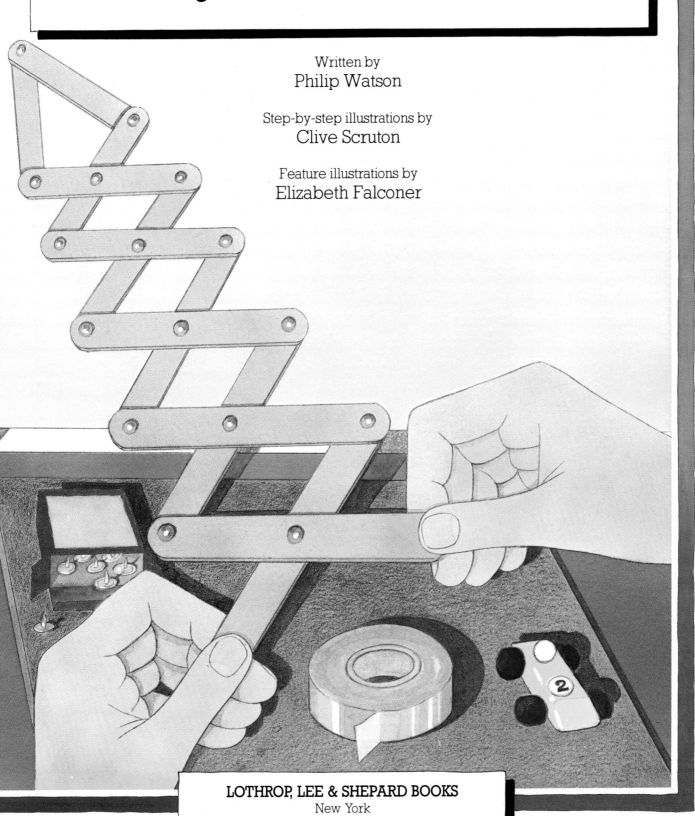

# Super Motion

Written by
**Philip Watson**

Step-by-step illustrations by
**Clive Scruton**

Feature illustrations by
**Elizabeth Falconer**

LOTHROP, LEE & SHEPARD BOOKS
New York

# Supplies and skills

## Basic materials

You don't need a lot of special equipment to experiment at home. Clear a special shelf or cupboard and start collecting some basic, inexpensive materials for your home laboratory.

Sheets of white and coloured paper and card.

Sheets of newspaper, brown paper or old wrapping paper.

Penknife, ruler and scissors.

Soft (B or 2B) and hard (3H) pencils.

Pair of compasses.

Elastic bands, string, cotton thread, paper clips, sticky tape and drawing pins.

## Other materials

If you are not familiar with a particular material or piece of equipment you need for an experiment, look for it in the following list.

**Acrylic paints** are sold at art and craft shops. You mix them with water, but when the paint dries it is water-proof.

**Batteries** are sold at electrical or radio shops. A battery's electrical energy is measured in volts. Electricity is taken from a battery via its terminals.

**Beads** are sold at haberdashers' and some craft shops.

**Bolts** are sold at hardware shops.

**Clingfilm** is a thin, transparent wrapping that sticks to surfaces. Buy it at a supermarket or grocery shop.

**Double-sided sticky tape** is sold at art or craft shops. It is sticky on both sides. One side is covered by paper, which you peel off.

**Dowelling** is like a round wooden stick. Buy it at a hardware shop.

**Flex, 1-core plastic-covered** is the kind that has strands of fine wire inside a plastic covering. Buy it at an electrical or radio shop.

**Insulating tape** is sold at electrical or hardware shops. It is thick and strong.

**Magnets** are made in several sizes and shapes. You can buy them in the science section of a large toy shop and in shops that sell parts for building radios. Loudspeakers for old-fashioned radios, gramophones and television sets used to have powerful 'permanent' magnets in them. Sometimes second-hand and junk shops sell this kind of magnet.

**Masking tape** won't leave a mark if peeled off gently. Buy it at an art or craft shop.

**A metal punch** can be bought at a hardware shop.

**A modelling knife** has a very sharp blade. Buy it at an art or craft shop.

**Nails** are sold at hardware shops.

**Nylon fishing line** can be bought from some sports shops or from shops that sell fishing tackle.

**Panel pins** are like nails with very small heads. Buy these at a hardware shop.

**Paper** is sold at stationery shops and at art or craft shops. You can use grease-proof paper instead of **tracing paper**.

**Pins** are sold at haberdashers' and department stores. **Straight pins** have heads. **Safety pins** are the type that can be closed.

**Plant pots and potting compost** are sold at garden centres and at flower shops.

**Pliers** are sold at electrical or hardware shops.

**Seeds and seed trays or pans** are sold at garden centres and at some flower shops.

**Softwood** is sold at hardware shops.

**A washer**, used in plumbing, is a small piece of metal with a central hole. Buy it at a hardware shop.

**Wire** can be bought at a hardware shop. **Galvanised wire** is coated with zinc and can be bent into any shape.

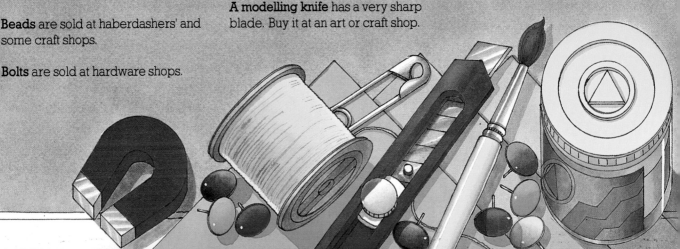

## Laboratory procedure

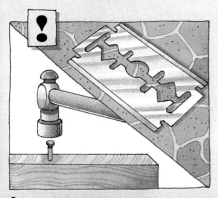

**1.** The exclamation symbol means that a tool (such as a metal punch), a material (such as a razor blade) or a process (such as hammering in a nail) can be dangerous. If you see this symbol on any part of an experiment, always ask an adult to read through the experiment with you before you start.

**2.** Put on old clothes, an overall or an apron before starting.

**3.** Read through an experiment, then collect the materials listed.

**4.** Clear a work area and cover it with newspaper or other paper. Put an old wooden chopping board or cork tile on the work area if you have to cut anything.

**5.** Take care not to get anything in or near your eyes. If this happens, immediately rinse your eyes in clean water, and tell an adult.

**6.** Never eat or drink anything unless told you may do so in an experiment.

**7.** Clean up any mess you make.

**8.** Wash your hands when you have finished an experiment.

## Drawing a circle

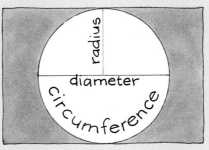

The radius is the distance between the centre of the circle and the circumference.
The diameter is double the radius.

**1.** Set the points of a pencil and a pair of compasses to the radius you require.

**2.** Put the point of the compasses firmly on a sheet of paper. It will mark the centre of the circle.

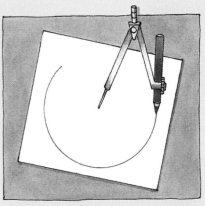

**3.** Swing the pencil round so that it draws a complete circle.

## Drawing diagonals

Diagonal lines join opposite corners at an angle. To draw diagonal lines, put a ruler at an angle between two opposite corners of a diagram.

**1.** Draw a straight line to join the opposite corners.

**2.** Repeat step 1 on the other two opposite corners.

The point where the diagonals cross is the centre.

## Checking right angles

Here are two ways to check that a right angle measures 90°.

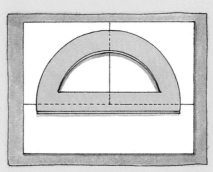

1. Put a protractor on one arm of the angle. The other arm should align with the 90° point on the protractor.

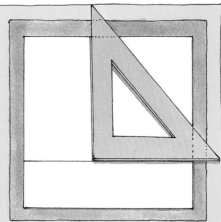

2. Put the 90° angle of a 90° set square on the point where the two arms meet. The arms should align with the edges of the set square.

# Good vibrations

When something vibrates, it moves rapidly to and fro. This kind of motion makes watches, clocks and many mechanical toys work. Vibrations also cause sound. Plucking a stringed instrument or tapping the prongs of a tuning fork sets up vibrations in the air, and this movement produces a musical note. The experiments in this chapter show some of the fascinating effects you can achieve with 'good vibrations'.

# Bouncing woodpecker

A home-made, vibrating spring sets this toy in motion. Watch the bird tap its way down the perch.

## Materials

- 1m dowelling about 1cm thick
- 30cm galvanised wire
- tracing paper 14cm × 8cm
- soft (2B) and hard (3H) pencils
- stiff, white card 14cm × 8cm
- scissors
- poster paints and paint brush
- clear sticky tape

**1.** Loosely twist one end of the wire three times round one end of the dowelling. This is the spring.

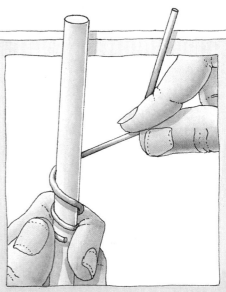

**2.** About 3cm from the last twist, bend the wire up at an angle.

**3.** Slide the spring off the dowelling.

**4.** Lay the tracing paper over the woodpecker in the large picture.

**5.** Trace the outline of the bird with the hard pencil.

**6.** Turn the paper over and shade across the lines with the soft pencil.

**7.** Lay the tracing paper, shaded side down, on the white card.

**8.** With the hard pencil, draw over the lines on the tracing paper.

**9.** Cut out the cardboard bird.

**10.** Paint one side of the bird. Let the paint dry, then paint the other side of the bird.

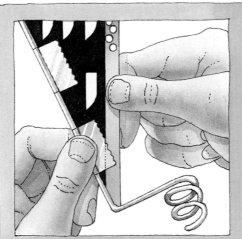

**11.** Tape the back edge of the bird's tail to the spring, as shown.

**12.** Slide the spring on to the dowelling again, bending the wire in or out so that the bird's beak will touch the dowelling.

The spring should bounce slowly down the wood. If it drops very quickly, tighten the coils. If it does not drop, loosen the coils a little.

## Making thunder

Sound travels more slowly than light, so you always hear thunder after you see a lightning flash. (Count the seconds between flash and rumble. Three seconds indicates that the lightning is about 1km away.) Make your own thunder by shaking a large sheet of cardboard or thin metal. This causes the air to vibrate and produce sound.

## Sonic boomer

This model makes a loud, cracking noise rather like a mini sonic boom. This happens because the moving paper causes the air to vibrate.

### Materials
- stiff card 20cm square
- lightweight, but strong paper 19cm square
- ruler and pencil
- scissors and clear sticky tape

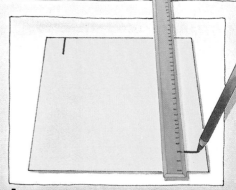

**1.** Mark points 2cm in from the top left-hand edge of the card, and 2cm up from the bottom right-hand edge.

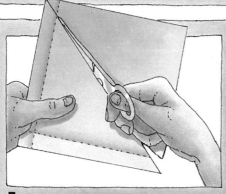

**7.** Cut along this diagonal line and discard the unfolded triangle.

**8.** Put the paper under the card.

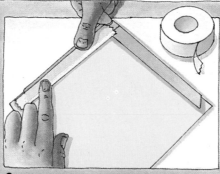

**9.** Fold the flaps on to the back of the card again, and tape them into position.

**10.** Turn the boomer right side up and carefully fold it in half. Pull the edge of a ruler down the fold to make a sharp crease.

## Private telephone

With this tin can telephone, you can speak to a friend some distance away. Your voice travels along the string between the cans more efficiently than through air. Use tin cans that have press-on lids. (Cans that have to be opened with a tin opener will have sharp edges.)

### Materials
- two clean, dry, empty tin cans with press-on lids removed
- about 25m fine string
- metal punch and hammer

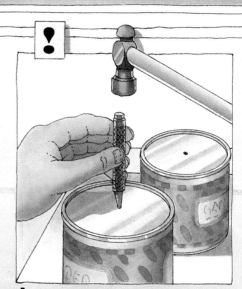

**1.** Ask an adult to punch a hole in the middle of the base of each can.

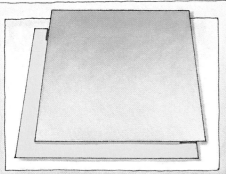

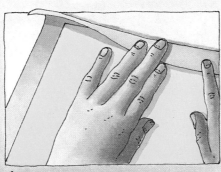

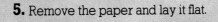

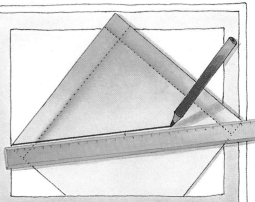

**2.** Lay the paper on the card so that two of its edges meet the 2cm-marks.

**3.** Turn the card over, holding the paper in position.

**4.** Fold the extending edges of the paper on to the back of the card.

**5.** Remove the paper and lay it flat.

**6.** Draw a diagonal line (see p.7) to join two corners, as shown.

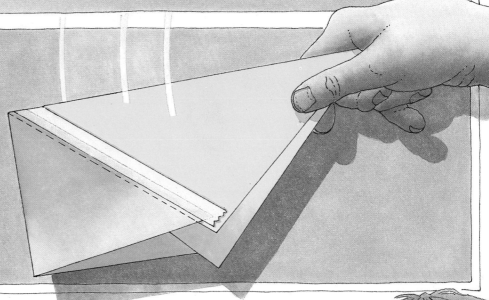

**11.** Hold the bottom corner of the boomer and quickly jerk down your hand.

As the paper is thrown out of the card, it pushes air aside, causing it to vibrate and make a loud crack.

**2.** Push one end of the string into the bottom of one can and tie a large knot in one end of it.

**3.** Fix the other end of the string into the second can in the same way.

**4.** Take the telephone outdoors and ask a friend to walk away with one can until the string is pulled tight.

**5.** Speak into your can while your friend listens to the other can.

Your voice causes the string to vibrate, and this vibration travels along the string to the other can.

**6.** If you pluck the string, you'll hear a very loud sound.

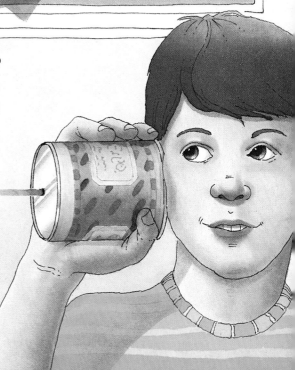

# Musical straws

Try this experiment to see how air can create different musical notes when it vibrates. Don't give up if you fail to get a note the first time you try. There's a knack to blowing through the straw.

## Materials

- 5 paper straws
- ruler and scissors
- clear sticky tape
- empty, tin can

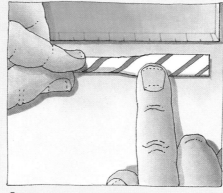

**1.** Flatten about 2.5cm of the tip of one straw with your finger.

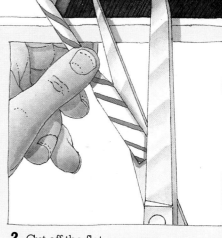

**2.** Cut off the flat corners.

**3.** Open the flat end slightly.

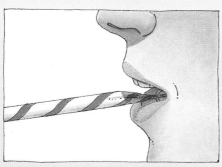

**4.** Dry your lips, put the flat end right into your mouth, and blow.

Air vibrating in the straw makes a note rather like the call of a duck.

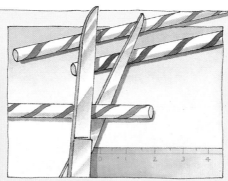

**5.** Cut 2cm off another straw, then cut each of the other straws 2cm shorter than the previous one.

**6.** Repeat steps 1-3 with these straws.

**7.** Blow into each straw.

The shorter the straw, the higher the note will be.

**8.** Blow each straw into the tin can.

When you blow, the flattened ends of the straw vibrate up and down in your mouth. This causes the air in the straw to vibrate too, creating sound. Blowing into the tin amplifies (makes louder) the sound, because the air in the tin is also vibrating. This effect is known as resonance.

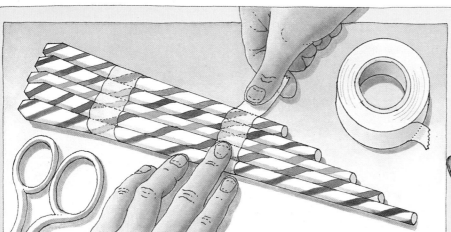

**9.** Gently tape the straws together in order of length, to make pipes.

When you blow into all the straws at once, you'll hear a chord.

**10.** Blow the pipes into the tin can.

## Notched record

You can see that a record is made up of circular grooves. With a magnifying glass, you can also see that each groove has notches cut in it, rather like the teeth of a saw. A moving record needle vibrates every time it hits one of these notches. This vibration produces sound, which is amplified through the loudspeakers.

## Picking up rhythm

This experiment shows how an early record player, or phonograph, worked. It had a funnel which amplified the vibrations that the needle picked up as the record turned under it. Be sure to use an old record that nobody wants, as this method of making sound could damage a good record.

### Materials
- paper 50cm square
- sticky tape
- fine sewing needle
- record player and old record

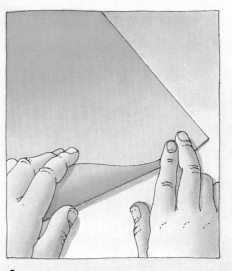

**1.** Curl over one edge of the paper, holding the corner flat.

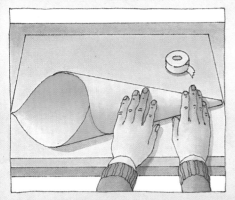

**2.** Keep rolling up the paper until you have a funnel-shape.

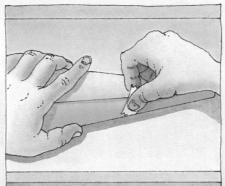

**3.** Use sticky tape to fix the loose edge of the paper.

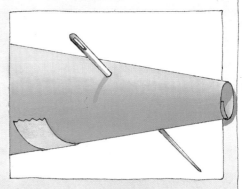

**4.** Push the needle through the funnel at an angle. It should be about 2cm from the pointed end.

**5.** Put the record on the turntable and start the record player at the correct speed.

**6.** Hold the wide end of the funnel and gently rest the needle on the record so that it points in the same direction as the record is moving.

If your hand is steady, you will hear the words and music on the record.

# Spinning motion

Think of all the things that work by spinning – bicycles, roller skates and frisbees, washing machines, clothes driers, electric mixers and film projectors are just a few. Many strange things can happen when materials start to spin. In this chapter, you can see some of the effects of spinning an elastic band, a twisted line, a raw egg and even ordinary water.

# Lunar buggy

The energy that makes this buggy move is stored in a wound-up elastic band inside the model.

## Materials

- 2 large, empty washing-up liquid bottles (the same size)
- modelling knife
- felt-tipped pen and ruler
- strong elastic band about 20cm long, unstretched
- 5cm and 30cm lengths strong wire
- pair of pliers and large washer

**1.** Cut off the base of one washing-up liquid bottle, then cut two 10cm-long tubes from the bottom end.

**2.** Draw lines 8cm long and about 2cm apart round each tube, then carefully slit along these lines.

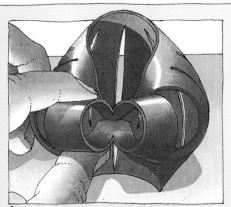

**3.** Fold the top and bottom strip of each tube inwards, to form a ring. This completes the buggy's tyres.

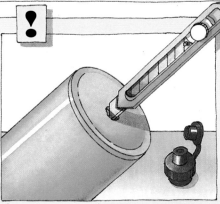

**4.** Cut (or pull) off the nozzle of the other washing-up liquid bottle, then cut a small hole in the centre of the base.

**5.** Push the tyres on to this bottle.

**6.** Use pliers to bend one end of the long piece of wire into a hook.

**7.** Push all but about 2cm of the elastic band into the hole in the base of the bottle.

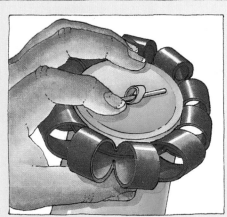

**8.** Put the short piece of wire through the loop of the elastic band, and hold it firmly against the base of the bottle.

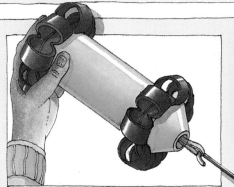

**9.** Put the hooked end of the long piece of wire into the bottle, to grasp and pull out the elastic band.

**10.** Hold the elastic band firmly, and remove the long piece of wire.

**11.** Slip the washer over the elastic band, then push about 5cm of the wire's length back through the loop.

**12.** Wind up the wire about 30 times and put the lunar buggy on the floor.

# Paddle boat

Paddle boats were once very common, and some are still in use today. They are driven by huge wheels, which are powered by steam. This model has a paddle wheel powered by energy stored in a wound-up elastic band. When the band unwinds, the wheel turns, pushing the water backwards and the boat forwards.

## Materials

- 2 lengths softwood, each 21cm × 1cm square
- block of softwood 15cm × 9cm × 2cm
- wood glue and hammer
- small cardboard box with lid
- four 2cm-long panel pins
- ruler, pencil and scissors
- lightweight, but strong card 32cm × about 8cm
- masking or insulating tape
- elastic band about 5cm long unstretched
- 2 washers, each 1-2cm in diameter, with holes of 4-5mm diameter
- acrylic paints and paint brush

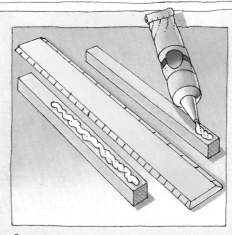

**1.** Spread glue down 15cm of one side of each length of softwood.

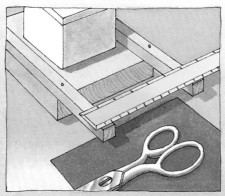

**5.** Measure the distance between the lengths of softwood, and cut the card 2-3mm less than this width.

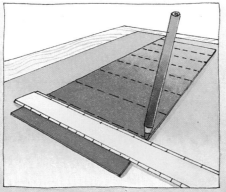

**6.** For the paddle wheel, mark points 4cm apart on both long edges of the card, then rule lines between them.

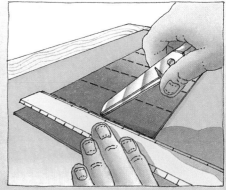

**7.** Guided by the ruler, pull the tip of the scissors along each pencilled line to score it.

**12.** Stand the paddle wheel on one end and paint it all over. You must do this, even if the card is coloured, to make it water-proof.
Let the paint dry.

**13.** Paint the top and sides of the deck and cabin.
Let the paint dry.

**14.** Put the elastic band over the middle of the paddle wheel.

**15.** Put a strip of tape right round each end of the paddle wheel to hold the four blades rigid.

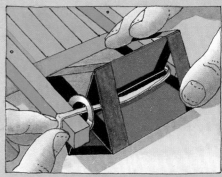

**16.** Pull one end of the elastic band through the hole in one washer, and pull this end of the band over one of the lengths of softwood.

**2.** Press the gluey sides to the long edges of the block of softwood.

**3.** Ask an adult to hammer two panel pins into each length to fix it firmly to the block of softwood.

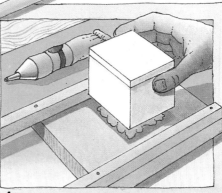

**4.** Glue the bottom of the cardboard box to the middle of the block, to form a deck and cabin.
Let the glue dry.

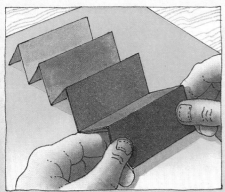

**8.** Fold the card alternately down and up along the score lines until it is folded into a concertina.

**9.** Hold the edges of the first fold together and join them with strips of tape.

**10.** Repeat step 9 on all the folds.

**11.** Tape the first and last folds together across the gap between them.

**17.** Repeat step 16 to fix the other end of the elastic band to the other length of softwood.

**18.** Wind up the paddle wheel about 10 times, then let it go.

It should spin fairly quickly. (If not, try using thinner washers.)

**19.** Now wind up the paddle 20 times and put the boat on water. Watch it paddle away!

# Spinning egg

This is an experiment which you may like to try first, and then show to a friend. You could make it into a game: 'pick out the raw egg'.

**Materials**
- unshelled, hard-boiled egg
- unshelled, raw egg

**1.** Put both eggs on a table, well away from the edge.

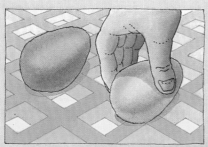

**2.** Spin each egg with your hand.

**3.** Briefly touch each egg to stop it, then quickly take away your hand.

The cooked egg, which is solid inside its shell, will stop spinning. When you stop the raw egg, the liquid inside is still spinning. When you take away your hand, the spinning liquid sets the egg in motion again.

# Lettuce drier

This experiment shows how a clothes spin-drier works – by pushing water out through holes in a rotating drum. Do the experiment when you want to make a salad.

**Materials**
- 2 colanders and cloth
- washed lettuce leaves
- ball of strong string
- scissors

**1.** Put the wet lettuce leaves in one of the colanders.

**2.** Tie the handles of the colanders together on one side.

**3.** Cut about 60cm of string and fold it in half.

# Mini yo-yo

When you throw down a yo-yo by its string, the toy always rises again. The spinning yo-yo winds the string back round itself. This mini yo-yo works on the same principle.

**Materials**
- 2 large, identical, lightweight buttons, each with 2 or 4 holes
- sewing needle and scissors
- reel of cotton thread

**1.** Thread the needle with about 30cm of cotton thread.

**2.** Hold the buttons with their smooth sides together.

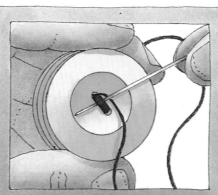

**5.** Push the needle under the threads on the outside of one button.

**6.** Tie a knot and trim the thread.

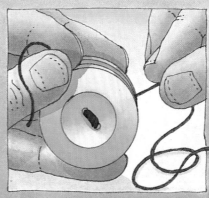

**7.** Wind about 70cm of extra thread once or twice round the thread between the buttons, and tie a knot.

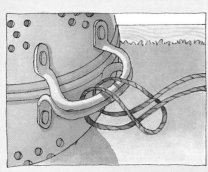

**4.** Put the looped end over the untied handles, and pull the ends of the string back through the loop.

**5.** Take the colanders outdoors.

**6.** Hold the ends of the string and spin the drier round for about 30 seconds.

When you untie the colanders, you will have dry lettuce for a salad.

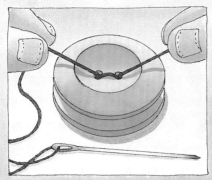

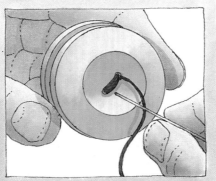

**3.** Push the needle and thread backwards and forwards through two opposite holes, then tie a knot.

**4.** Sew the buttons together by pushing the needle and thread through the holes several times.

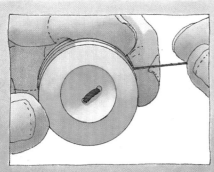

**8.** Pull the thread tight and wind all of it round the centre threads.

**9.** Tie a finger-sized loop in the end of the thread.

**10.** Put your finger in the loop and flick the yo-yo down. Then jerk up your hand to make the yo-yo rise.

# Water overhead!

Show your friends how to stop water falling out of an upside-down bucket! You'll astonish everyone with this trick that makes water seem to defy the force of gravity.

### Materials
● small, plastic bucket half-filled with water

**1.** Take the bucket outdoors.

**2.** Gently swing it from side to side in front of you, to establish a rhythm.

**3.** Quickly swing the bucket in a circle over your head.

When you swing the bucket, the water is forced away from you. So even when the bucket is over your head, there's no danger of getting wet!

## Spinning pin

Here's a way to balance a drawing pin on its point. With your hand resting on a table, hold the pointed end of the pin between your thumb and one finger. Spin (or twist) it out of your hand so that it falls on the table on its spinning point. You'll see that it spins away, perfectly balanced.

## The acrobat

This acrobat is quite an entertainer, and will somersault backwards and forwards as you stretch or slacken the line from which he dangles.

### Materials

- tracing paper about 20cm square
- soft (2B) and hard (3H) pencils
- lightweight card 10cm × 8cm
- ruler and scissors
- poster paints and paint brush
- pair of pliers
- two 3cm-lengths fine wire
- straight or safety pin
- 8 small, round beads
- 2 beads, each about 0.5cm long or about 8 small, round beads
- 30cm nylon fishing line
- 2 lengths softwood, each 25cm × 1cm square
- 1 length softwood 10cm × 1cm square
- 2 nails about 1.5cm long
- hammer
- 4 drawing pins

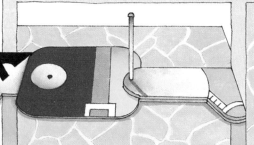

**9.** Hold the legs on either side of the body and use the pin to pierce through all the pieces of card.

**10.** Repeat step 9 for the arms.

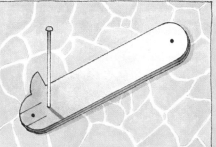

**11.** Make two pinholes, about 0.5cm apart, in the tips of each hand.

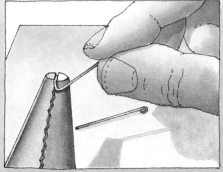

**12.** Use pliers to bend one end of each length of wire into a tight loop. The loop will hold the beads on the wire.

**17.** Ask an adult to nail the short piece of softwood between the long pieces, about 8cm from the ends. The bar is at the *bottom* of the frame.

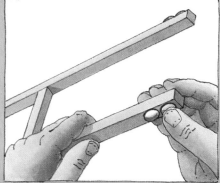

**18.** Push two drawing pins into each outer edge of wood at the top of the frame. The drawing pins should just touch each other.

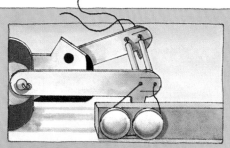

**19.** Put the looped end of the nylon line round both drawing pins on one arm of the frame.

**20.** Tie the ends of the line round the other pair of drawing pins. It should be tight enough to pull the arms of the frame together slightly.

**1.** Lay the tracing paper over the patterns for the acrobat's body, one arm and one leg.

**2.** Trace the patterns with the hard pencil. Trace the leg and arm twice.

**3.** Lift off the paper, turn it over, and shade across all the traced lines with the soft pencil.

**4.** Lay the tracing paper, shaded side down, on the card.

**5.** With the hard pencil, draw over the lines on the tracing paper.

**6.** Draw over the outlines with pencil, if they are not clear.

**7.** Cut out the shapes.

**8.** Paint the shapes on one side. Let the paint dry, then paint the other side of each shape.

**14.** Bend the end of the wire into a loop and clip off any extra wire.

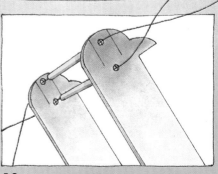

**13.** Thread one round bead on to one length of wire, add one leg, then a bead, then the body, then a bead, then the other leg, then a bead.

**15.** Using the other length of wire, repeat steps 13 and 14 to fix the top of the arms to the body.

**16.** Push the nylon line through one hole in one hand, add a long bead, then push the line through the opposite hole in the other hand. Repeat with the other pair of holes.

If you have tied the line correctly, there should be half a twist in it when the frame is held upright with the acrobat dangling below the line.

**21.** Holding the bottom of the frame, gently squeeze together, then release, the arms of the frame.

The acrobat will do somersaults. This happens because the stretching force of the arms on the line cause it to keep twisting and untwisting, throwing the acrobat backwards and forwards.

# Natural rhythm

Our world is full of movement. The earth itself turns on its axis once a day. That's how we get day and night. It circles the sun once a year, creating the different seasons. All the animals and plants that live on the earth move, too – some in curious ways. Your body also moves in a very special way. Dip into this chapter, to see the variety of motion in the natural world.

# Burrowing worms

Worms are active and useful workers. They help farmers by mixing and breaking up soil as they burrow through it. You can study the way in which worms move by making a special worm house for them. Don't keep the worms for more than a month – return them to the wider world of a garden or park.

## Materials

- large, glass jar with screw-top, metal lid
- metal punch and hammer
- cardboard tube as tall as jar
- clingfilm or plastic
- damp garden soil and old spoon
- sand, if possible
- about 4 earthworms
- few small leaves
- sheet of brown paper
- elastic band

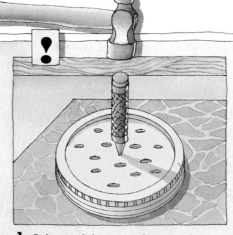

**1.** Ask an adult to punch several small holes in the lid of the jar.

**2.** Cover the cardboard tube with the clingfilm (or plastic). (The tube will keep the worms nearer the glass where you can see them.)

**3.** Hold the tube in the jar and put a deep layer of soil round it. Add worms as you find them.

**4.** Add a thin layer of sand.

**5.** Repeat steps 3 and 4 until the jar is almost full.

**6.** Put the leaves on top of the soil.

**7.** Screw on the lid.

**8.** Wrap the brown paper round the jar and secure it with the elastic band. The worms will be in darkness, just as they are underground.

**9.** Put the jar in a cool place for a few days.

**10.** Unwrap the brown paper and take off the lid.

You will see that the worms have mixed together the soil and sand. Look for burrows that they have made, and for the leaves, which they often use to plug their burrows. You may also see some worm casts on the surface. These are the tube-like remains of soil that the worms eat with their food, and which later pass through their bodies.

**11.** Every few days, add a little water to the soil in the jar.

## Moving eye

The pupil (or black centre) of your eye is, in fact, a hole. By expanding and contracting, the pupil controls the amount of light entering your eye. To see this, stand very close to a mirror in a darkened room. Shine a torch on your face, and then look quickly at one pupil. You will see it shrink rapidly.

## Sensitive plants

Flowers such as Livingstone Daisies (*Mesembryanthemum criniflorum*) open their petals in daylight and close them at night. A Sensitive Plant (*Mimosa pudica*), on the other hands, folds up its leaves if you touch them. You can grow either plant, and then watch its behaviour. Whichever plant you choose, sow the seeds at the end of winter, and give spare seedlings to your friends.

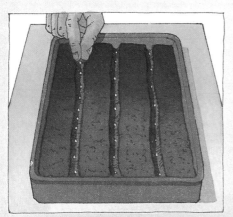

**4.** Sow the seeds about 2cm apart in the furrows.

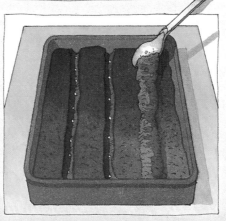

**5.** Gently spoon a very thin layer of compost over the seeds.

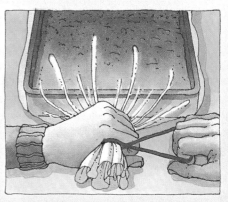

**6.** Put the tray into the plastic bag, then close the bag by winding the elastic band round the opening.

**12.** Gently use the spoon to dig one seedling from the tray.

**13.** Put the seedling into the hole prepared in one pot.

**14.** Scoop compost round the seedling, then firm the compost with a finger.

**15.** Repeat steps 12-14 to transplant three more seedlings.

**16.** Put Livingstone Daisies outdoors in a sunny position. (Eventually, you could plant them in a window box or garden, as these plants spread.)

Look at the Daisies in the early morning or late evening.

You'll see the petals of the flowers opening and closing.

## Materials

- shallow seed tray or pan
- potting compost
- watering can and water
- packet of Livingstone Daisy or Sensitive Plant seeds
- old tablespoon
- large, plastic bag
- elastic band
- 4 plant pots about 7cm diameter
- small pebbles or pieces of broken crockery

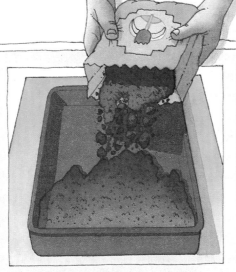

**1.** Fill the tray with compost to within about 2.5cm of the top.

**2.** Use your finger to make two or three furrows, each about 2mm deep, in the compost.

**3.** Water the compost very lightly.

**7.** Put the tray in a light, warm place for about two weeks. Don't put the tray in direct sunlight, and keep the soil moist.

**8.** When the seedlings are about 4-5cm high, take off the plastic bag. Do this the day before you are ready to transplant the seedlings into pots.

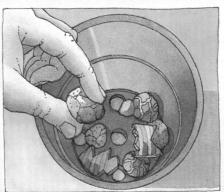

**9.** Cover the drainage holes of the pots with the small pebbles (or pieces of broken crockery).

**10.** Fill each pot with compost to within about 2cm of the top.

**11.** Water very lightly, then dig a hole in the compost in each pot.

**17.** Keep Sensitive Plants indoors in a well-lit place, but not in direct sunlight. Keep them moist and feed them fertiliser occasionally. (Give them larger pots, eventually.)

When the plants are strong and healthy, gently touch the leaves.

They will fold together and the leaf stalks will droop down. Leave the plant undisturbed, and gradually the leaves will unfold and stand upright.

26

# Active roots

The roots of plants grow downwards because they are attracted to the earth by the invisible force of gravity. This is called geotropism. You can watch a plant's roots change direction in this experiment.

## Materials
- small, glass jar with about 2cm of water in it
- blotting paper and scissors
- 2 or 3 runner bean seeds

**1.** Cut the blotting paper to fit inside the jar, and put it in.

**2.** Put the bean seeds between the paper and the wall of the jar.

**3.** Leave the jar in a warm, dark place.

In a few days, you will see the bean roots growing downwards.

**4.** Gently lift out the blotting paper and the seeds.

**5.** Replace the blotting paper.

**6.** Turn the seeds upside down, then repeat steps 2 and 3.

In a few more days, you will see that the roots have changed direction!

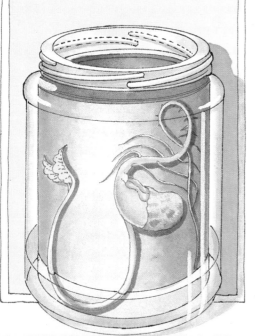

# Night movements

Some animals are active in daylight, others at night. With this simple device, you can see insects in action on a spring or summer's evening.

## Materials
- cardboard box about 40cm square
- small torch
- modelling knife
- masking tape
- tracing paper about 40cm square

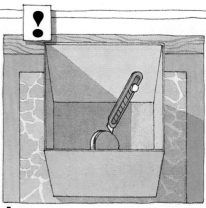

**1.** Cut a hole in the centre of the base of the box. It should be the same diameter as the torch barrel.

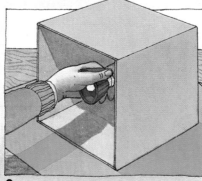

**2.** From the inside of the box, slide the barrel end of the torch through the hole until only the bulb part of the torch is inside the box.

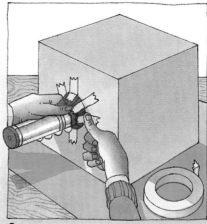

**3.** Tape the barrel to the outside of the box.

**5.** In the evening, put the box outdoors and switch on the torch. Leave the box for 15 minutes.

A number of insects, such as moths, will crowd on to the tracing paper screen. (You could use a reference book to identify them.) The insects are instinctively attracted to any light source.

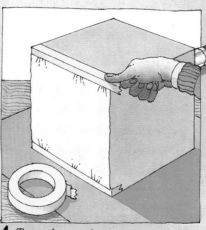

**4.** Tape the tracing paper over the open side of the box.

# Body rhythm

Blood is moved round your body by your heart, which beats regularly as it pumps the blood. You can find out how regularly your heart beats by taking your pulse. If you do this experiment, you can also *see* your pulse beat! Ask someone to find the pulse for you.

## Materials
- drawing pin
- dead match-stick
- clock or watch with second hand

**1.** Gently push the blunt end of the match-stick on to the point of the drawing pin.

**2.** Ask someone to find the pulse in your left wrist, and balance the head of the drawing pin on it.

The match-stick will move gently from side to side, as the blood is pumped through your veins.

**3.** Count how many times the match-stick wobbles in one minute. This is your pulse rate.

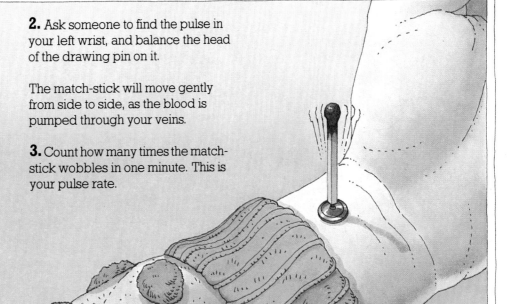

# Impossible movements

Because we have a good sense of balance, we can move about quite easily. But there are certain movements which, although they seem simple, we are unable to do. Ask some of your friends to do this experiment with you for fun.

**1.** Stand against a wall, with your feet together and one shoulder and one hip touching the wall.

**2.** Keeping your outside leg straight, try to lift it sideways.

**3.** Stand against a wall, with your feet together and your back and heels touching the wall.

**4.** Keep your legs straight and try to touch your toes.

**5.** Stand about 30cm from a wall. Rest your head on the wall, keeping your body perfectly straight and your arms by your side.

**6.** Now try to stand up straight.

## Our sun

The sun seems to rise in the east, travel across the sky, and set in the west. You can observe this on any sunny day. But it is not the sun that moves – it is the earth. The earth revolves once every 24 hours, and it is this movement that causes our sun to appear to move.

## Sundial

If you make a sundial, you can tell the time by the sun's position, which seems to alter as the earth spins on its axis. A sundial is easy to use – as long as the sun is shining! You can take it on camping holidays or on walks, and always be able to tell the time without looking at a watch.

### Materials

- block of white softwood 20cm square × 2cm thick
- ruler and soft (2B) pencil
- ballpoint pen
- 15cm galvanised wire
- pair of pliers
- hammer and nail
- compass or materials as for 'Home-made compass' (see pp.40-41)
- clear plastic about 21cm square
- masking or insulating tape

**6.** Mark the half-way point on the unbordered edge of the wood, and draw a line in ballpoint pen across the thickness of the wood.

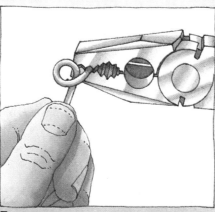

**7.** Use the pliers to bend one end of the wire into a small loop.

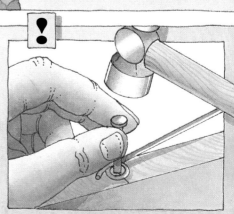

**8.** Ask an adult to nail the looped end of the wire to the wood at the half-way point. You should be able to push the wire sideways.

**15.** Repeat steps 13 and 14 every hour on the hour.

**16.** At sunset, bring the block of wood and compass indoors.

**17.** With the ballpoint pen, write the time that each line represents in the border.

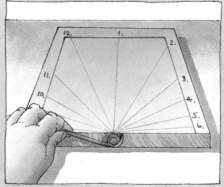

**18.** Push down the wire into a horizontal position.

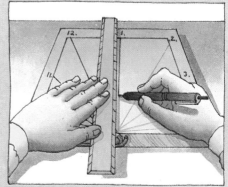

**19.** Using the ballpoint pen, neatly rule over each shadow-line.

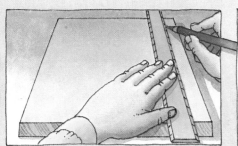

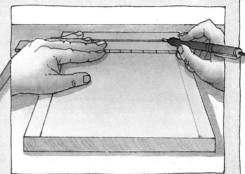

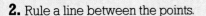

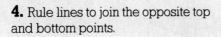

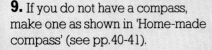

**1.** Measure 2cm down from one edge of the wood. Mark points, making sure that they are also 2cm in from the parallel sides.

**2.** Rule a line between the points.

**3.** Mark points 2cm from each corner on the opposite edge of the wood.

**4.** Rule lines to join the opposite top and bottom points.

**5.** Following the pencilled lines, and using the ballpoint pen and ruler, draw in a 2cm-wide border on three sides of the wood.

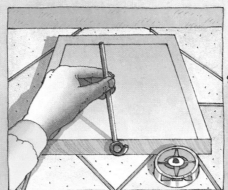

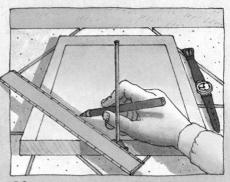

**9.** If you do not have a compass, make one as shown in 'Home-made compass' (see pp.40-41).

**10.** Early on a bright, summer's day, take the block of wood and compass outdoors.

**11.** Use the compass to position the wood so that the edge fixed with the wire faces south (if you are in the northern hemisphere) or north (if you are in the southern hemisphere).

**12.** Adjust the wire so that it sits vertically, and lines up with the half-way point marked in ballpoint.

**13.** When a clock indicates the hour, lightly pencil in the shadow on the wood so that it meets the border.

**14.** Write the hour in the border.

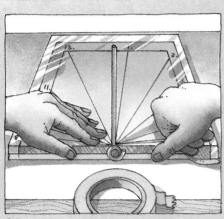

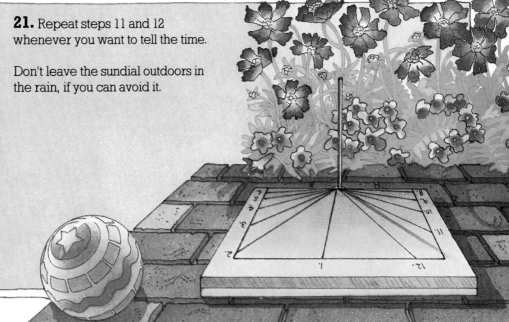

**20.** Push the wire into a horizontal position, and tape the clear plastic over the top of the sundial.

**21.** Repeat steps 11 and 12 whenever you want to tell the time.

Don't leave the sundial outdoors in the rain, if you can avoid it.

# In the balance

When you balance a ruler on your finger, it's as if the whole weight of the ruler is centred at one point above your finger. This point is called the centre of gravity. For any object to balance, its centre of gravity must be directly above or below the balancing point. Because the earth's gravity pulls things down, a moving object always comes to rest when its centre of gravity is as low as possible. The experiments in this chapter show how to achieve a state of perfect balance!

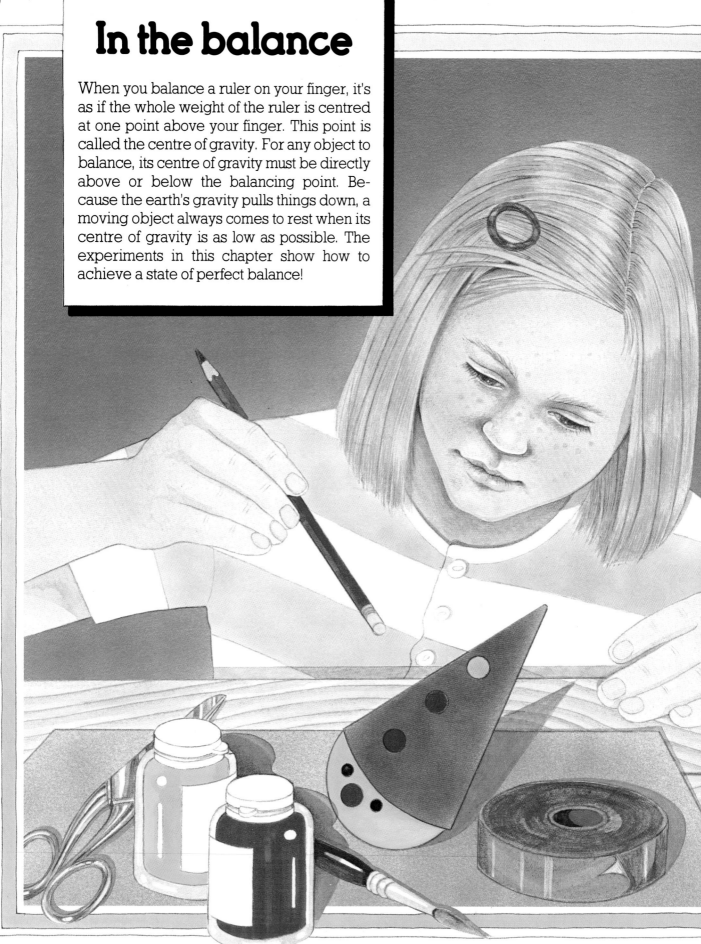

# Noddy clown

This toy refuses to be knocked over, however many times you tap it! It simply rocks from side to side.

## Materials
- table tennis ball
- modelling knife and pencil
- thin 'sausages' of plasticine
- coloured paper 10cm square
- scissors and sticky tape
- poster paints and paint brush

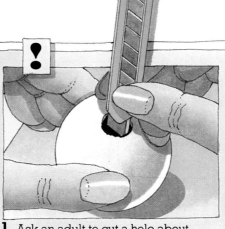

**1.** Ask an adult to cut a hole about 0.5cm in diameter (see p.7) in the top of the ball. Shake out any loose bits.

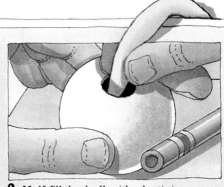

**2.** Half-fill the ball with plasticine, packing it down evenly with the blunt end of the pencil. The plasticine must be distributed evenly.

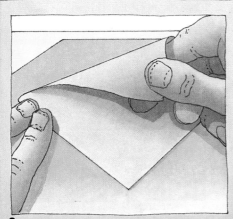

**3.** Hold one corner of the paper and fold it round and round to make a narrow, pointed funnel.

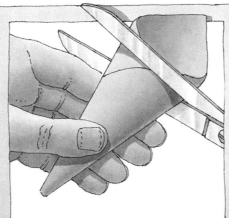

**4.** Holding the loose outside flap in position, cut across the funnel to make a straight edge.

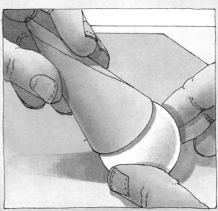

**5.** Put the open end of the funnel on the ball, letting the paper uncurl until it fits tightly over the ball.

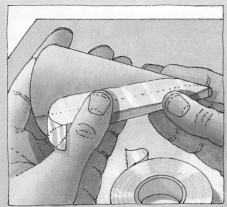

**6.** Use sticky tape to fix the outside flap into position. This completes the hat.

**7.** Put the hat back over the ball and give it a gentle tap.

The model will swing backwards and forwards without falling over.

The toy clown swings because most of its weight is near the ground. This means that its centre of gravity is very low, which is the best position for good balance.

**8.** Paint the cap and ball all over. Let the paint dry, then add the clown's nose, mouth and eyes.

### Tricky lift

When you next have the opportunity, watch how a workman lifts a step-ladder off the ground. He will grasp the ladder near its centre, because then there will be an equal distribution of weight on both sides of his hands. Try lifting a small ladder by holding one end of it. Which is the better way to lift a ladder?

## Tight-rope walker

To balance well on a wire, most of the weight of an object should be below the wire. That's why tight-rope walking is so skilful – most of the performer's weight is above the wire and has to be evenly distributed to give balance. This model tight-rope walker works so well because his weight is in the ideal position.

### Materials

- tracing paper about 12cm square
- soft (2B) and hard (3H) pencils
- white card about 12cm square
- scissors
- poster paints and paint brush

**6.** Pencil over the pattern on the card, if you cannot see all the lines clearly.

**7.** Carefully cut out the cardboard figure. (Don't forget to cut the notch in one foot.)

**8.** Paint the figure on one side. Let the paint dry.

**9.** If you have a length of wire, go on to step 11.

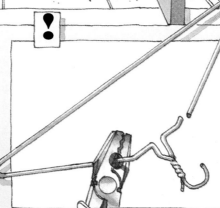

**10.** If you are using a coat-hanger, ask an adult to cut off the hook and then straighten the wire hanger.

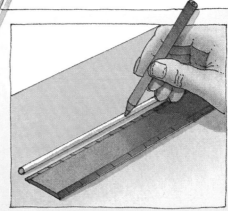

**11.** Measure and mark a point 8cm from one end of the wire.

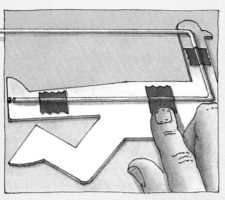

**15.** Tape the wire frame to the back of the cardboard figure, as shown.

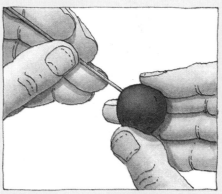

**16.** Push the ball of plasticine on to the end of the wire.

**17.** Tie one end of the nylon fishing line to a curtain rail or cupboard handle in your room.

**18.** Tie the other end of the line to a fixed point on the opposite side of the room, so that the line slopes downward.

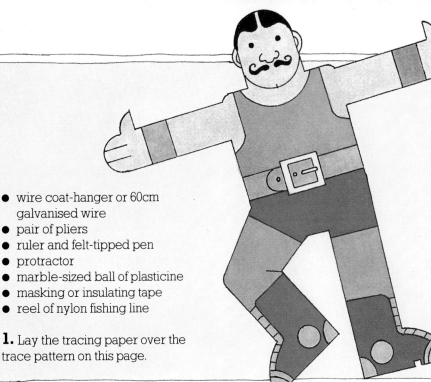

- wire coat-hanger or 60cm galvanised wire
- pair of pliers
- ruler and felt-tipped pen
- protractor
- marble-sized ball of plasticine
- masking or insulating tape
- reel of nylon fishing line

**1.** Lay the tracing paper over the trace pattern on this page.

**2.** Trace the lines of the pattern with the hard pencil. (Note that there is a notch in one foot.)
Lift off the tracing paper.

**3.** Turn the paper over and shade across all the traced lines with the soft pencil.

**4.** Lay the tracing paper, shaded side down, on the white card.

**5.** With the hard pencil, draw over the lines on the tracing paper.
Lift off the tracing paper.

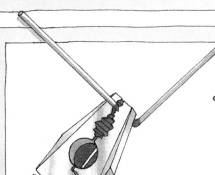

**12.** Use the pliers to make a 90° angle (see p.7) at the 8cm-point.

**13.** On the longer arm of the wire, measure and mark a point 4cm from the right angle.

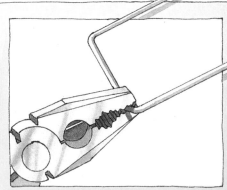

**14.** Use the pliers to make another right angle at this 4cm-point, as shown.

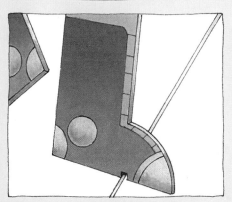

**19.** Position the notch in the figure's foot on the line.

Your tight-rope walker will slide down the line, perfectly balanced. Most of his weight is in the ball of plasticine. As the force of gravity pulls things down, this weight is in the ideal position when it is as low as possible.

# Balancing needle

You might think it's impossible to balance a needle on its point, but this experiment shows how it can be done very simply.

## Materials
- sewing needle
- cork
- 30cm galvanised wire
- small potato

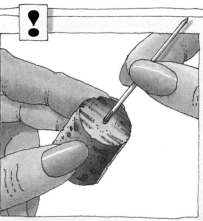

**1.** Ask an adult to push the blunt end of the needle into the top of the cork.

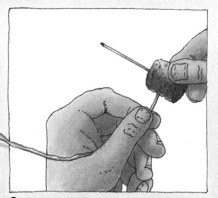

**2.** Bend the wire into a semi-circle and push one end of it into the side of the cork.

**3.** Push the other end of the wire into the potato.

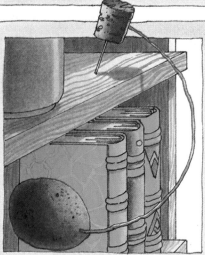

**4.** Rest the pointed end of the needle on the edge of a shelf.

Amazingly, the needle balances, even if you gently swing the potato. You can see that most of the weight of the model is below the point of the needle. In scientific words, the model's centre of gravity is low. This is the state in which any object will be perfectly balanced.

# Swinging parrot

This very decorative parrot is so perfectly balanced that it will never fall off its perch unless disturbed.

## Materials
- tracing paper 30cm × 15cm
- soft (2B) and hard (3H) pencils
- white card 30cm × 15cm
- scissors
- poster paints and paint brush
- ball of plasticine (green, if possible) about 2cm in diameter

**1.** Lay the tracing paper over the trace pattern of the parrot and its stand.

**8.** Paint one side of the parrot and its stand. (Paint the stand the same colour as the front of the parrot.) Let the paint dry.
Then paint the other side of the parrot and the stand.
Let the paint dry.

The colours of the bird shown are those of an Amazon Parrot. You can use other colours, if you like.

**10.** Push the ball of plasticine on to the end of the bird's tail.

**2.** Trace the outlines of the patterns with the hard pencil. Don't forget to trace the dotted lines.
Lift off the tracing paper.

**3.** Turn the paper over and shade across all the traced lines with the soft pencil.

**4.** Lay the tracing paper, shaded side down, on the white card.

**5.** With the hard pencil, draw over the lines on the tracing paper.
Lift off the tracing paper.

**6.** Pencil over the outlines on the card, if they are not clear.

**7.** Cut out the shapes, then cut along both dotted lines.

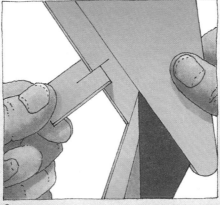

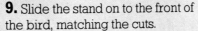

**9.** Slide the stand on to the front of the bird, matching the cuts.

**11.** Stand the parrot on a shelf and gently tap its head.

If it does not swing perfectly, add or subtract plasticine.

The plasticine adds weight to the parrot. When you swing the model, you raise the level of the plasticine. But all weights always try to reach the lowest level possible, because they are pulled downwards by the force of gravity. So the parrot will swing until the plasticine weight is at its lowest point again.

# Pulling power

The forces of electricity and magnetism make objects move in lots of interesting ways. You can't see the force fields that surround electric currents and magnets, but you can study some of their amazing effects by doing the experiments in this chapter. Static electricity causes certain particles to jump about. Magnets attract ferromagnetic metals, such as iron and steel, as if by magic.

# Magnetic sculpture

Magnets attract objects made of iron and steel, the size and number of the objects depending on the strength of the magnet. One of the delights of this experiment is that you can change the sculpture you make with the magnet whenever you like.

## Materials
- 3 or more powerful magnets
- paper clips, nails, ball bearings, washers or other metal objects

**1.** Put the magnets on a table and move them about until the ends are attracted to each other.

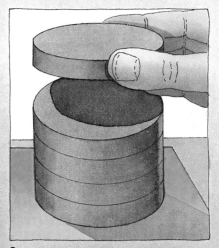

**2.** Now stack the magnets in a column, with their attracting ends together.

**3.** Arrange the metal objects on the magnets.

# Dancing metal

This experiment shows how iron or steel will dance about when it is close to, but not touching, a magnet.

## Materials
- large, flat magnet
- 20cm wood about 1cm square
- strong glue and ruler
- cardboard box, such as a cereal box, with one open end
- nails or panel pins or small objects made of iron or steel

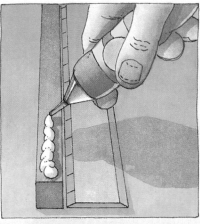

**1.** Spread a little glue over about 5cm of one end of the wood.

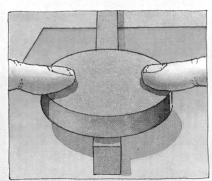

**2.** Press the magnet to the gluey end of the wood. Let the glue dry.

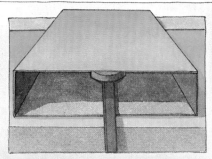

**3.** Put about half the length of the wood into the open end of the box.

**4.** Put the nails on top of the box, roughly above the magnet.

The magnet exerts a pulling force on the nails, even though it does not touch them. So the nails will be held in a fixed position on the box.

**5.** Move the length of wood sideways or in and out of the box.

The nails will follow, like dancers to music.

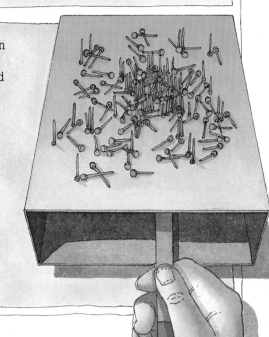

## Magnetic attraction

Here are two quick experiments that show a magnet's power to attract a metal object. Remember, the stronger the magnet, the larger the object it will attract.

### Materials
- bar or horseshoe magnet
- safety pins or paper clips
- glass of water and nail

**1.** Pick up one closed safety pin (or paper clip) with the magnet. Make a chain by attracting more pins (or clips) to the first one.

**2.** Drop a nail into a glass of water. Move the magnet up the outside of the glass, pulling out the nail without even touching it!

## Racing magnets

Magnets are not always attracted to each other. One magnet may move away quite rapidly from another, as you will see in this amusing experiment. Magnets behave like this because they have two very different ends, or 'magnetic poles'.

### Materials
- 3 small, circular magnets

**1.** Stack the magnets so that they all stick together.

**2.** Lift off the top magnet and put it on the table, keeping it facing the same way up.

**3.** Repeat step 2 with the second magnet.

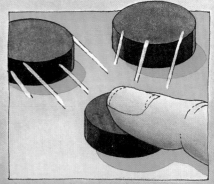

**4.** Put your finger on one magnet and slide it towards the other two.

You'll find that the magnets race away from each other.

**5.** Turn over the magnet under your finger and repeat step 4.

Now the magnets cannot resist racing towards each other!

All magnets have a north and a south pole, just as the earth does. The poles are on opposite ends of bar magnets; they are on the ends of the arms of horseshoe magnets, and on opposite edges of circular magnets. A north pole and a south pole attract each other. (We say 'opposite poles attract'.) Two north or two south poles always move away from each other (or 'like poles repel').

## Swinging magnet

See how one magnet makes dramatic movements, as it feels the pulling power of three others.

### Materials

- tall, cardboard box at least 10cm deep and 10cm wide
- ruler and pencil
- sewing needle
- pair of compasses
- 4 small, circular magnets
- strong glue and sticky tape
- scissors and reel of cotton thread

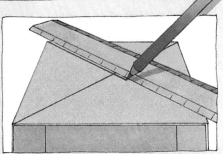

**1.** Stand the box on one end and draw two diagonal lines (see p.7) to join the opposite corners of its top.

**2.** Turn the box upside down and repeat step 1 on the bottom end.

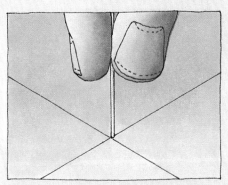

**3.** Make a needle hole in the centre of both the top and the bottom, so that you can see the centres on the inside of the box.

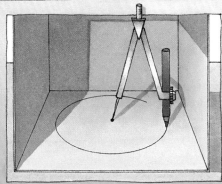

**4.** Put the point of the compasses in the hole in the bottom inside, and draw a 4cm-radius circle (see p.7).

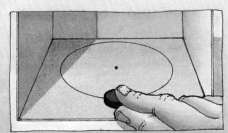

**5.** Stack the magnets so that they stick together, then detach one.

**6.** Put a dot of glue on the base of this magnet, then press it on the circumference (see p.7) of the circle.

**7.** Repeat step 6 with the next two magnets, spacing them evenly round the circle.

**8.** Cut a 5cm-length of thread and tape it in a loop to the top of the spare magnet.

**9.** Cut a thread longer than the height of the box and tie it to the looped thread on the magnet.

**10.** Thread the needle with the end of the long thread.

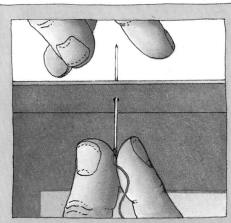

**11.** Starting from inside the box, push the needle and thread through the hole in the top of the box.

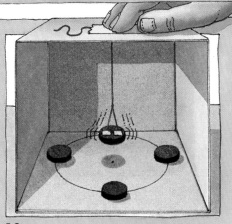

**12.** Tape the thread to the outside of the box so that the magnet hangs about 3cm above the centre of the circle. Remove the needle.

**13.** Swing the suspended magnet.

Because opposite poles are facing each other, the suspended magnet is attracted to each of the three magnets on the base as it swings past them. This makes it jerk about. As the length of the swing decreases, the magnet will be suddenly drawn to one of the steady magnets.

## 🔖 Home-made compass

The earth, with its North and South Poles, is like a huge magnet. That's why a compass needle always points north. You can magnetize metal and make your own compass. Ask an adult to help, as there are sharp tools and materials in this experiment.

**Materials**

- small, round, plastic box with lid such as a typewriter ribbon box
- razor blade
- strong, flat magnet
- cork tile or part of cork tile
- pair of compasses and pencil
- ruler and modelling knife
- straight pin and pair of pliers
- masking or insulating tape
- push-on top of ballpoint pen
- scissors and sheet of white paper
- double-sided sticky tape
- coloured pencils (optional)

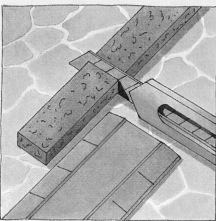

**1.** Measure and cut off a piece of cork about 3cm × 1cm.

**7.** On the paper, draw a circle with a circumference (see p.7) about 0.5cm less than that of the base of the box.

**8.** Cut out the paper circle.

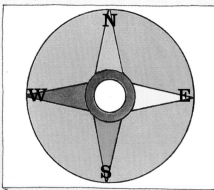

**9.** Copy this diagram on to one side of the paper circle. Colour the points, if you like.

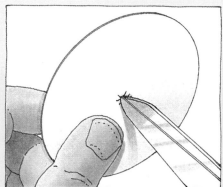

**10.** Guided by the mark left by the point of the compasses, make a small hole in the centre of the paper.

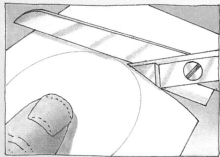

**13.** Balance the razor blade on the pen-top tip in the box.

The blade will point north-south. If you are familiar with the area you live in, you should know which end is north and which is south.

**14.** Take the blade off the pen-top tip and mark 'N' on it to indicate its north pole.

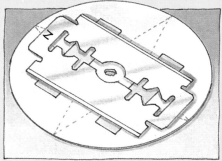

**15.** Press the razor blade to the sticky tape on the back of the paper circle. The N on the blade must align with the N pointer.

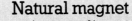

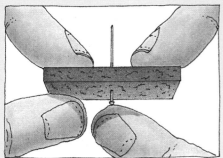

**2.** Push 1.5cm of the pin through the middle of the cork.

**3.** Use pliers to cut off the head end of the pin so that the bottom of the cork is perfectly flat.

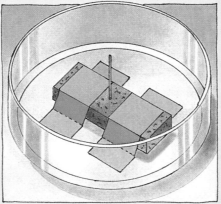

**4.** Use masking (or insulating) tape to tape the cork to the middle of the base of the box.

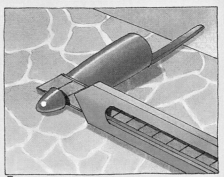

**5.** Cut off the very tip (about 1cm) of the ballpoint pen top.

**6.** Put the tip on the point of the pin. It should swing freely.

**11.** On the back of the paper, put small strips of double-sided sticky tape on opposite sides of the hole, then peel off the backing paper. Put the paper circle aside.

**12.** With the magnet, slowly stroke the razor blade about 30 times in the same direction. Lift the magnet clear away after each stroke.

The razor blade is now magnetized. If you have stroked the blade with the north pole of the magnet, the end of the blade where you began stroking will also be the north pole. The same applies to the use of the south pole of the magnet. (See 'Racing magnets' pp.38-39 to find out about magnetic poles.)

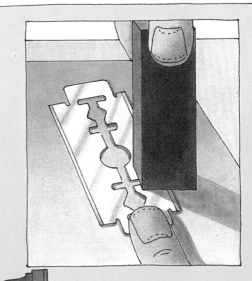

**16.** Balance the blade and paper on the pen-top tip.

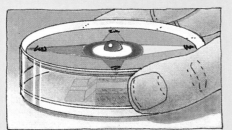

**17.** Put the lid on the box to protect the compass.

### Natural magnet

Lodestone is a type of iron ore that is naturally magnetic. The Vikings were the first people to make a simple compass using lodestone. If you magnetize a large nail (see step 12 above) and tie cotton thread to each end of it so that it can be suspended horizontally, it will act like an early Viking compass did.

# Aladdin's lamp

If you have a small fluorescent light tube at home or at school, ask an adult to take it out of its socket to do this experiment.

## Materials
- small fluorescent light tube
- cellophane food wrapping

**1.** In a dark room, rub the cellophane wrapping over the tube.

It will glow eerily because you have charged the glass with static electricity. This attracts electrons, which are tiny parts of an atom, inside the tube. The special white coating on the inside of the tube produces light when the electrons hit it.

## Jumping cereal

Static electricity can attract some unusual particles. To see this, put a thin layer of breakfast cereal on a sheet of aluminium foil, then put a clear plastic box (5-10cm deep) over the cereal. Vigorously rub the box with a woollen cloth. The cereal will jump about, attracted by static electricity in the plastic box.

# Electric grab

By making electricity pass round a coil of wire, you can produce quite a strong magnet. Scientists call such a device an electromagnet. Electromagnets are used in scrap yards to lift cars, and on docks to lift large pieces of iron and steel. When the electricity is switched off, the electromagnet drops its load. Here's a simple switch-operated electromagnet to use at home.

## Materials
- 6m standard 1-core plastic-covered flex
- ruler and felt-tipped pen
- bolt 8-10cm long
- insulating tape and scissors
- 4.5 volt battery with screw terminals
- block of softwood 10cm × 15cm × 2cm
- length of softwood 30cm × 3cm × 1cm
- 2 drawing pins and paper clip
- nails, keys or other metal objects

**1.** Measure and mark points 1.5m apart along the flex.

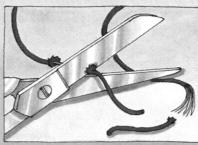

**6.** Strip about 2cm of plastic from both ends of the flex.

You will find lots of fine strands of shiny wire underneath.

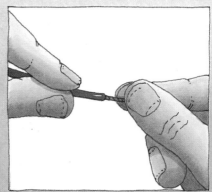

**7.** Twist these fine strands into single strands on both ends of flex.

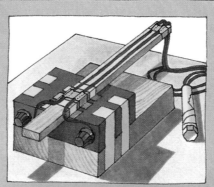

**11.** Tape the flex to the length of softwood in two places: close to the terminals and at the end of the wood, as shown.

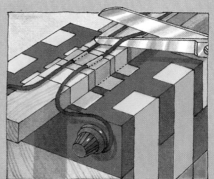

**12.** Cut one of the lengths of flex 3cm from the tape near the terminals.

**13.** Repeat steps 6 and 7.

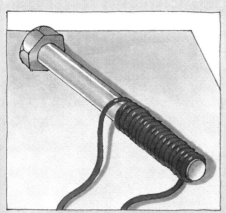

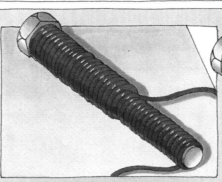

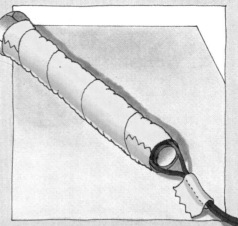

**2.** Starting from one of the marks on one end, wind the flex in tight coils round the bolt, as shown.

**3.** Wind to the next 1.5m mark, then wind the flex back down the bolt. Stop when you reach the last mark.

**4.** Wind insulating tape round the flex on the bolt to hold it.

**5.** Tape the lengths of flex together about 0.5cm from the end of the bolt.

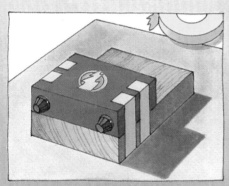

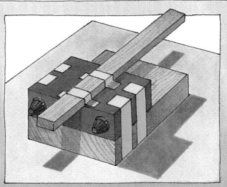

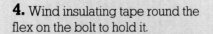

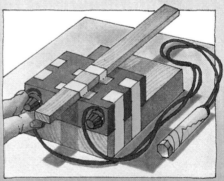

**8.** Tape the battery to the block of softwood, with the terminals at one end of it.

**9.** Tape the length of softwood to the battery so that about 5cm overhangs at the terminals.

**10.** Loosen the battery screws, then wind each wire round one screw. Tighten the screws.

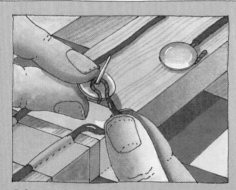

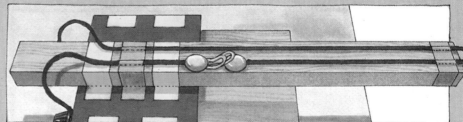

**14.** Wind each wire round a drawing pin under its head, and gently press the drawing pins, 1-2cm apart, into the wood.

**15.** To make the switch, slightly bend up one half of the paper clip. Pull out the drawing pin near the battery, put the flat part of the clip under it, and press the pin into the wood. The bent end of the clip should be just above, but not touching, the other drawing pin.

To switch 'on', press down the clip so that it touches the drawing pin. Release the clip to switch 'off'. Switch on and off to pick up and drop metal objects in the house or garage. Imagine how useful your electromagnet will be if anyone drops a key into a drain!

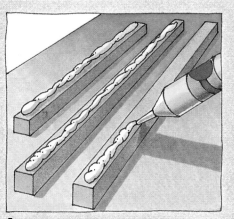

## Magnetic car

This is an amusing game that works by magnetic attraction. All magnets are surrounded by a magnetic field, which can exert an influence through cardboard and other materials. In this experiment, you also make a telescopic arm, which is great fun.

**Materials**
- stiff, white card 50cm × 70cm
- toy car
- ruler and pencil
- coloured pencils or felt-tipped pens
- 50cm-length of wood 1cm square
- 2 lengths of wood, each 70cm × 1cm square
- strong glue
- 12 flat lolly sticks
- insulating tape and scissors
- cork tile and modelling knife
- 13 drawing pins and 13 small beads
- 2 small, circular magnets

**1.** Spread glue on one edge of each length of wood.

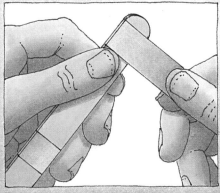

**5.** Wind the tape round the ends and middle of each lolly stick. Put two sticks aside.

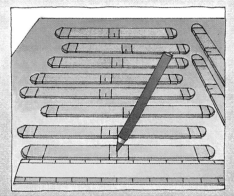

**6.** Measure and mark the centre of the other 10 sticks.

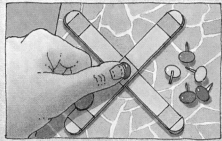

**7.** Working on the cork tile, make an 'x'-shape with two lolly sticks, and push a drawing pin into their centres.

**8.** Repeat step 7 with the other eight lolly sticks.

**14.** Tape one of the magnets just behind the drawing pin at the pointed end of the arm.

**15.** Find and mark the opposite (or attracting) pole of the other magnet. (See 'Racing magnets' pp.38-39.)

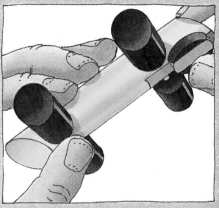

**16.** Tape the magnet, marked side up, underneath the car at its front end.

**17.** Put the car on the card.

**18.** Put the telescopic arm under the card, with the magnet below the car.

**19.** Squeeze, then pull apart, the telescopic arm to make the car move.

If you are skilful, you can guide the car round the race track.

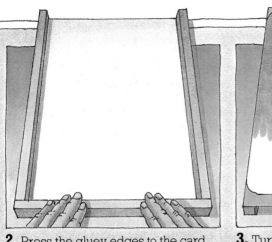

**2.** Press the gluey edges to the card in a 'u'-shape, as shown. Let the glue dry.

**3.** Turn the card over and draw a race track on it. Colour the track.

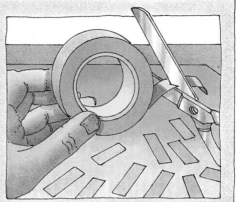

**4.** For the telescopic arm, cut 36 strips of tape, each about 4cm long.

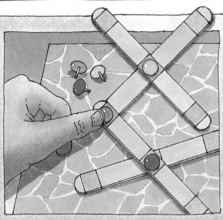

**9.** Join the five 'x'-shapes by pushing a drawing pin through each of the ends of two adjoining sticks.

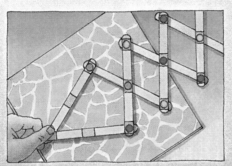

**10.** Join one end of each of the two spare lolly sticks to the ends of the arm, then join their ends.

**11.** Put a bead on each pin-point.

**12.** Put tape over each bead.

**13.** Test the arm by holding two sticks on one end and squeezing them together, then pulling them apart.

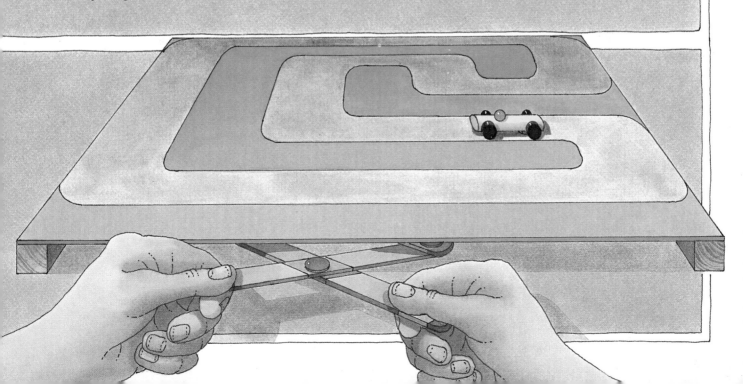

# Glossary and index

Words in CAPITAL LETTERS are also defined in the glossary.

### amplify
To make SOUND louder. *see pp.12-13*

### balance
Condition of an object at rest, when its centre of GRAVITY is directly above or below the point on which the object is pivoted.
*see pp.20, 27, 30-31, 32-33, 34-35*

### compass
A small MAGNET which can swing freely, and which always comes to rest pointing north-south.
*see pp.28-29, 40-41*

### electromagnet
Type of MAGNET powered by electricity. *see pp.42-43*

### electrons
Tiny, active particles inside an atom. All matter, or the material that makes up the universe, consists of atoms.
*see p.42*

### geotropism
Movement of plant roots towards the earth, due to the pull of GRAVITY.
*see p.26*

### gravity
An invisible force surrounding the earth, which causes objects to be attracted to the earth.
*see pp.19, 26, 30, 33, 35*

### gravity, centre of
The point at which the weight of an object seems to be concentrated. When an object is perfectly balanced, its centre of GRAVITY is directly above or below the balancing point.
*see pp.30-31, 32-33, 34-35*

### magnet
An object which has the property of attracting certain metals. Every magnet has two ends, or 'magnetic poles'. If suspended freely, the north pole of a magnet will always point to the north pole of the earth, and the south pole will always point south.
*see pp.36-37, 38-39, 40-41, 42-43, 44-45*

### resonance
Effect caused by VIBRATION of an object inside a container, which can AMPLIFY SOUND by making particles of air vibrate around it. *see p.12*

### sound
Effect caused by VIBRATION of an object, which sets up waves in the surrounding air. *see pp.10-11, 12-13*

### spring
A simple mechanical device, usually made of coiled metal. *see pp.8-9*

### static electricity
The opposite of 'current' (or moving) electricity. 'Static' means 'at rest'. When static electrical particles build up on a body, the body will attract smaller objects such as fluff or hair. *see p.36, 42*

### stored energy
Energy waiting to be released – in a wound-up elastic band, for instance.
*see pp.14-15, 16-17*

### sundial
Instrument for measuring time by the position of the sun. *see pp.28-29*

### vibration
A rapid movement backwards and forwards. *see pp.8-9, 10-11, 12-13*